DOMINOES

The Drive
to Dubai

LEVEL TWO   **700 HEADWORDS**

OXFORD
UNIVERSITY PRESS

Great Clarendon Street, Oxford OX2 6DP

Oxford University Press is a department of the University of Oxford.
It furthers the University's objective of excellence in research, scholarship,
and education by publishing worldwide in

Oxford New York

Auckland Cape Town Dar es Salaam Hong Kong Karachi
Kuala Lumpur Madrid Melbourne Mexico City Nairobi
New Delhi Shanghai Taipei Toronto

With offices in

Argentina Austria Brazil Chile Czech Republic France Greece
Guatemala Hungary Italy Japan Poland Portugal Singapore
South Korea Switzerland Thailand Turkey Ukraine Vietnam

OXFORD and OXFORD ENGLISH are registered trade marks of
Oxford University Press in the UK and in certain other countries

© Oxford University Press 2010

First published in Dominoes 2004

2022

14

ISBN: 978 0 19 424892 1 BOOK
ISBN: 978 0 19 463965 1 BOOK AND AUDIO PACK

No unauthorized photocopying

Printed in China

This book is printed on paper from certified and well-managed sources.

ACKNOWLEDGEMENTS

Cover image reproduced with permission from: Getty Images (truck in desert/Olaf Loose).

Illustrated by: Paul Collicutt

The publisher would like to thank the following for permission to reproduce photographs: Alamy
Images p26 (Dubai architecture/Robert Harding Picture Library Ltd); Getty Images pp19
(Dubai waterfront/Nevada Wier); Oxford University Press pp41 (palm trees at sunset/
Photodisc), 48 (skyscraper windows/Photodisc), 54 (video camera/infografick); Shutterstock
pp12 (car in desert/Seqoya), 18 (gold bangles/oleandra), 59 (Middle Eastern businessman
talking on the phone/zeljkodan).

DOMINOES

Series Editors: Bill Bowler and Sue Parminter

The Drive to Dubai

Julie Till

Illustrated by Paul Collicutt

Julie Till was born and grew up in Liverpool in the north of England. She has lived and worked in the Middle East for over twenty years as a journalist, a teacher, an author, and a teacher-trainer. She has run workshops for teachers in many countries including Yemen, Syria, Egypt, and Morocco. Her husband is Lebanese and they have one son. She now lives in Dubai, but often travels for work. She enjoys speaking Arabic as she travels around the countries of the Middle East. In her free time she likes to read.

OXFORD
UNIVERSITY PRESS

BEFORE READING

1 Sheikh Ahmed Bin Salem gave some jewellery to his wife last year. This year it was stolen. Who took it? Tick one box.

a **Khaled Mansoor:** he works for Sheikh Ahmed Bin Salem.

d **Marcia Cruz:** one of the women who cleans Sheikh Ahmed Bin Salem's house.

b **Abu Malek:** he works for Sheikh Ahmed Bin Salem, making tea and coffee in the office.

e **Abdul Umar:** one of the men who cleans Sheikh Ahmed Bin Salem's office building.

c **Omar Bin Salem:** Sheikh Ahmed Bin Salem's son; he has an Internet business.

f **Hussein Al-Hussein:** a man from a very important family.

2 Kareem and Samira try to find the thief. Why? Tick one box.

Kareem Mansoor, Khaled's son. He is a student.

Samira Al-Hussein, Hussein's daughter. She is a student, too.

a ☐ Because they are studying to be police officers and they hear about the stolen jewellery through Kareem's father.

b ☐ Because the police think that Kareem's father Khaled stole the jewellery and Samira wants to help Kareem.

c ☐ Because the police think that Samira's father Hussein stole the jewellery, and Kareem wants to help Samira.

CHAPTER 1
Happy times

It was the best week of my life. Only seven days, but seven good days. And then the trouble began. But I'd like to tell you about the good days first. On Saturday my father came home and told us about his new job.

'You're looking at the new **Financial Manager** at the Eastern **Trading Company**. More money, a company car and a driver,' he said, smiling at us.

We were very happy to hear the news. My father worked very hard, day after day, week after week, year after year to get this new and important job. When other **employees** arrived at the office in the morning, my father was already on his second cup of coffee. At night, only the **cleaners** saw my father leave. Even when he took a week's holiday, he had work with him. Nobody worked as hard as my father. Now, after twelve years of hard work, he was at the top.

That evening we held a little party at our home for our family and friends. They all came, happy to hear our good news. When the bad times came, they stopped visiting, but for that first week everything was wonderful. Now my father had his new job, my family and the family of Samira Al-Hussein agreed to meet. They were going to talk about a possible **engagement**.

I liked Samira a lot. She had a wonderful smile and friendly eyes. Her father was a very rich and important man, but she was kind and friendly to everyone. My family agreed that she would be a good wife and mother. But did Samira's family think I could be a good husband for her?

My mother and sister often met Samira and her family at **weddings**. My sister told me Samira could sing and dance better than any of the other girls. She also told me that my mother often talked to Samira's mother about me:

Financial Manager a person who works with the money in a business

trade to buy and sell

company a business

employee a person who works in a business

cleaner a person who tidies a building and washes the floors

engagement when two people tell their friends that they are going to marry

wedding the day when two people marry

'Kareem is a good son and very clever. He knows everything about computers. His teachers think that he's one of their best students.'

'I'm sure Kareem will get a very good job after he finishes and then he'll want to marry a nice girl.'

My mother was right. I was working hard for my **exams**, but every Wednesday I left the **university** a little earlier than usual and drove past the place where Samira was a student. On Wednesdays Samira finished early and she waited for her family's driver outside the front building. I never stopped and talked to her in front of her friends, but I drove very slowly past them. Her friends laughed at me, but I wasn't angry with them. Samira smiled at me and I felt happy.

Her friends laughed at me.

My **parents** met only once before their wedding, but I wanted to know Samira better. I got Samira's **mobile phone** number from my friend's sister and we often talked and sent **text messages** to each other. She was funny and clever. The more I talked to Samira the more I liked her. But did she like me as much as I liked her? I wasn't sure.

The evening before an important exam, she sent me a text message. I opened it. There was a picture of a heart. It made me feel hopeful. Now I needed good **exam results**. Two days after my father started his new job I got them. I had the best exam results in the university. It was time to ask. I told my father that I wanted to **get married**. He called my mother to tell her the news, but she already knew.

'Your son wants to get married. He wants to marry Samira Al-Hussein.'

I could never surprise my mother, but she often surprised me. She has always known what I wanted – and tried to get it for me!

My father was not sure. 'Samira's a very nice girl, but she comes from a rich family. Her father is **Minister of Telecommunications**. Perhaps her family won't agree,' he said.

'I know father, but you have an important job and now I have my exam results I can get a good job, too. I know Samira's mother likes my mother very much. And I think that Samira likes me,' I said, suddenly looking down at my feet.

'I think she likes you too,' my mother said, smiling. 'Her mother asks questions about you every time we meet.'

My father was still not sure. 'Why do you want this girl? She comes from a really important family, you know. There are lots of other nice girls from good families.'

'But I don't want another girl. I want to marry Samira. She's beautiful, clever, and kind. There's no other girl that I want to marry,' I said.

parent a mother or a father

mobile phone a phone that you can carry with you

text message a note in writing, sometimes with pictures, that you can send from one mobile phone to another

exam results the number of questions a student gets right

get married to marry

Minister of Telecommunications the important person who makes decisions about telephones and television in a country

3

By the end of the evening, with my mother's help, my father agreed to meet with Samira's family.

⌒

Two days later my parents went to see Samira's parents. They were both wearing their best clothes and my mother was wearing her best **jewellery**. The driver arrived in the new company car and at a quarter to seven they left the house. I phoned Samira at once. She knew all about the meeting.

'I talked to my mother about you,' she laughed. 'I talked and talked and talked. I told her all about you. Of course she knows your family and she thinks that your parents are nice. I asked her to talk to my father about you. I'm sure that my mother will agree to the engagement, but I'm not sure about my father.'

Samira had two older married sisters and two younger brothers, but Samira was her father's favourite child. He wanted her to marry a rich man, a man from an important family like himself. I tried to sound happy, but I was worried.

It was the longest three hours of my life. Luckily, Samira phoned me from time to time with news about the meeting. She was listening in the next room, her ear against the door. She could hear most of what our parents were saying.

'My father asked your father about his new job and now they're talking about your exam results. My father thinks that you're very clever . . . Now they're talking about what job you could take.'

At five past nine she phoned me again.

'It's going very well. They're laughing. I think that they're talking about me, but I can't hear what they're saying.'

Ten minutes later another phone call.

'Everything is OK. Your parents are leaving. My father said yes. There will be an **announcement** about our engagement on Saturday and we can get married after I finish university. Oh, I must go. I can hear my mother calling me.'

But Saturday came and there was no announcement.

jewellery
expensive things that people wear, like gold rings

announcement
when you tell everyone about something important, for example an engagement

She could hear most of what our parents were saying.

READING CHECK

Are these sentences true or false? Tick the boxes.

		True	False
a	A young man called Kareem is telling the story.	☑	☐
b	Kareem's father has a good job.	☐	☐
c	Kareem wants to marry a young woman called Samira.	☐	☐
d	Samira comes from a poor family.	☐	☐
e	Kareem's father talks to Samira's father about their children marrying.	☐	☐
f	Kareem's father thinks that marrying a woman from an important family is a good idea.	☐	☐
g	Kareem sees Samira every day.	☐	☐
h	Samira's parents have only one child.	☐	☐

WORD WORK

1 These words don't match the pictures. Correct them.

a ~~jewellery~~
text message

b wedding

. . . .

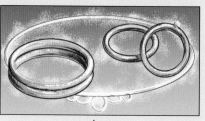

c cleaner

. . . .

d text message

. . . .

2 Find words in the boxes to complete the sentences.

a Oxford is a famous u n i v e r s i t y in England.   YIVNSURIET

b Kareem wants to get good e _ _ _ r _ _ _ _ _ _ .   AXME SUTELSR

c After finishing his studies, Kareem tells his father that he wants to
g _ _ m _ _ _ _ _ _ .   TEG DIERRMA

d In some countries p _ _ _ _ _ _ find the woman that their son will marry.   SNAEPRT

e Kareem's father is a f _ _ _ _ _ _ _ _ _ m _ _ _ _ _ _ .   LACNIFANI RAGAMEN

f He has worked for years in the Eastern T _ _ _ _ _ _ C _ _ _ _ _ _ _ .   GNITARD ANOPCYM

g Samira's father is the M _ _ _ _ _ _ _ _ of   SIRMENIT CMOOSMTUENAICIETNL
T _ _ _ _ _ _ _ _ _ _ _ _ _ _ _ _ _ _ .

h Kareem and Samira will have a party for their e _ _ _ _ _ _ _ _ _ _ .   MEGTEGNAEN

i Samira's father will make an a _ _ _ _ _ _ _ _ _ _ _ _ about his daughter
and Kareem.   CNOMUNEENTNA

GUESS WHAT

What happens in the next chapter? Tick two sentences.

a ☐ Kareem's father goes to Dubai.
b ☐ Kareem's father comes home late that evening.
c ☐ Kareem decides not to marry Samira.
d ☐ Kareem's father has a car accident.
e ☐ Kareem's father dies.
f ☐ Kareem's father has problems with the police.

CHAPTER 2
Waiting

The day after the meeting with Samira's parents, my father told us that he was travelling to Dubai the next morning. We were surprised. There was nothing strange about travelling to Dubai, but on a Friday? During the week he was very busy, but on Fridays he liked to stay at home with his family. My father explained that he had some important business for the **owner** of his company, Sheikh Ahmed Bin Salem. He had to go tomorrow.

My father often travelled to Dubai these days. Sheikh Bin Salem had another company there. My father usually went there for him. Sometimes he went to other places and met other people. Sheikh Bin Salem **trusted** my father. He trusted him more than any of his other employees.

The next morning my father was ready at ten to six. Ten minutes later his driver arrived. My father finished his coffee, said goodbye and left. It was a long journey. Many people like to stay one night in Dubai and travel home the next day. But not my father. He doesn't like hotels. He prefers travelling all day and arriving home late at night.

Just before lunch, father phoned. My mother was busy in the kitchen so I answered the phone. My father told me that they were already in Dubai. He said that he didn't have much to do there. He would be home between nine and ten o'clock that evening.

Ten o'clock came and went. At first we weren't worried. Perhaps there was a lot of traffic on the roads. At eleven o'clock my mother said to us, 'Your father's very late. I'm surprised he hasn't called. I think I'll phone him and find out what the problem is.'

Five minutes later she came back into the room, looking worried.

owner the person that something belongs to

trust to think that someone will do what is right and good

8

'There's no answer. His phone is off.'

'Perhaps he forgot to **charge** it,' said Amira, my sister.

'But why is he so late? I'll wait until midnight. If he's still not home, I'll phone the police,' said my mother.

Half past eleven and no sound of a car. Quarter to twelve, nothing. At five to twelve my mother couldn't wait any longer.

'There's something wrong. I know it. He's never this late.' She looked at me. 'Go and ring the police, Kareem. Perhaps there's been a car accident.'

She turned to one of my younger brothers. 'Ibrahim, phone your uncle in Dubai. Tell him your father isn't home yet. Ask him to phone the hospitals there.'

She told my sister Amira to look for our father's **address** book. She wanted to speak to the driver's family. We phoned many people that night. We found the driver's phone number and spoke to the driver's family. They knew nothing. They were also very worried. They had family in Dubai, too, and they phoned them. Their family also phoned the police and the hospitals. But there was no news about my father or the driver.

The next day my mother phoned Samira's mother. We could not make an announcement about the engagement until we found my father. It was not right. Samira's family agreed. Her father said he would help us to find him. He knew many people here and in Dubai.

So we waited and waited. But there was no news. My mother sat next to the phone all day. She didn't eat. She slept for only three or four hours that night. Early next morning, I found her next to the phone again, sitting and waiting. She looked so worried. Then, around lunch time, there was a phone call. It was someone who knew Samira's father. He was phoning from Dubai. He had good news. We thought that it was good news, because he told us my father was alive.

'Where is he?' asked my mother.

charge to put electricity into

address where somebody lives

9

We couldn't hear what the man was saying, but my mother looked surprised.

'What's he doing there? Has there been an accident? Did the driver hit someone?' she asked. My mother listened, **nodding** her head from time to time. At the end of the call she put the phone down and looked at us.

'Your father's alive,' she told us. 'Thank God, he's alive.'

'Where is he? What's happened?' asked Ibrahim.

'He's at a **police station**. I don't know what's happened. There's some kind of a problem. He didn't have a car accident, but the police want to ask him questions. I'm going to phone your uncle and ask him to go to the police station now. He can phone us when he knows more,' said my mother.

Two hours later there was another phone call. My mother listened for a long time. She looked very worried.

'What's the matter, mother? What's happened?' I asked.

'I don't understand. The police think that your father's a thief. They say that he stole jewellery from Sheikh Bin Salem's wife.'

'Father's not a thief. How can they say this?' said Amira.

'It must be a mistake,' I said.

'What's going to happen now?' asked Ibrahim.

'Your uncle has spoken to Sheikh Bin Salem. He's driving to Dubai. He'll be there in a few hours. He'll talk to the police. Your uncle's waiting at the police station. I'm sure everything will be fine,' said mother, putting her arm around Amira.

We sat by the phone all day, waiting for a call from my uncle. Hour after hour we waited. Suddenly, around two o'clock in the afternoon, the phone rang. Four hands shot out. My mother was the quickest. She put the phone to her ear. At first she said nothing. From time to time she nodded her head. She put the phone down and looked at us.

nod to move your head up and down

police station the building where the police work

'The driver has already left the police station. But the police still think that your father stole the jewellery. They think that he was trying to sell it to a man in Dubai. They want to put

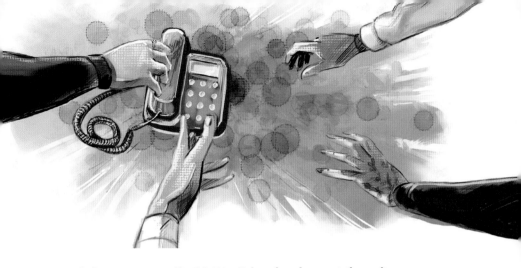

your father in prison. Sheikh Bin Salem has been at the police station all day. He told them that he doesn't want your father to go to prison. He told them that he loves your father like a brother. Thank God for that!' she cried.

Four hands shot out.

'So what's going to happen?' asked Ibrahim.

'The police have got most of the jewellery. They haven't got his wife's **diamond necklace** or her **ruby earrings**, but Sheikh Bin Salem doesn't want your father to go to prison.'

'So when's father coming home?' I asked.

'In a day or two, I think. The police want to ask him some questions first. They want the rest of the jewellery.'

The house felt strange without my father. Each time we heard a car we ran to the front door. It wasn't him. Then, two days later, a taxi arrived in front of the house. My father got out of the car. He looked older, thinner. His head was down. We ran to him and put our arms around him as the car drove away.

We went into the house. My parents went into my father's office and closed the door. Even with the door closed, we could hear my mother crying. We couldn't hear what my father was saying. His voice was very quiet. The door opened and my father called us.

'Please come in. I want to speak to you all.'

diamond a very expensive stone that usually has no colour

necklace you wear this around you neck

ruby a very expensive stone that is usually red

earring jewellery that you wear in your ear

11

READING CHECK

Put these sentences in the correct order. Number them 1–9.

a ☐ Kareem's mother finds that her husband's phone is off.

b ☐ Kareem's father goes to Dubai.

c ☐ Kareem's mother phones Samira's mother.

d ☐ Kareem's father comes home.

e ☐ Kareem's uncle phones with news.

f ☐ Kareem's father phones to say that he will be home between nine and ten o'clock.

g ☐ Kareem's brother Ibrahim must phone his uncle in Dubai.

h ☐ Sheikh Bin Salem arrives in Dubai.

i ☐ Kareem's family phones the driver's family.

WORD WORK

Complete the sentences on page 13 with words from the picture below.

a Sheikh Bin Salem .... *trusts* .... Kareem's father.

b Sheikh Bin Salem is the .... of the Eastern Trading Company.

c .... and .... are very beautiful, very expensive stones.

d You wear a .... round your neck.

e You wear .... in your ears.

f Kareem's father is in a .... in Dubai where they are asking him questions.

g When you don't .... your mobile phone, you can't use it.

h When a friend of Samira's father phones from Dubai, Kareem's mother doesn't speak a lot, but she .... from time to time.

GUESS WHAT

What happens in the next chapter? Tick the boxes.   Yes   No

a Kareem's father talks about what happened in Dubai.   ☐   ☐

b Kareem's father goes to prison.   ☐   ☐

c Kareem gets married to Samira.   ☐   ☐

d Kareem's father must stay at home for a time.   ☐   ☐

CHAPTER 3
Father's story

My father was standing near the window. My mother was sitting in a chair, looking at him. My father spoke to us first.

'I'll say this only once. I am not a thief. I don't know who stole the jewellery, but it wasn't me.'

'Of course your father isn't a thief, but people will talk. You must be strong and not listen to them,' said my mother.

'What happened father? Why do the police think that you stole the jewellery,' asked Amira.

'About two weeks ago, somebody stole a watch, a necklace, some earrings and two rings from Sheikh Bin Salem's house. They were very expensive. The police asked Sheikh Bin Salem and his wife to give them the names of all their visitors. They have a lot of visitors. I've been a visitor there many times as you know. They gave my name but the police didn't ask me any questions. Nobody thought that I was a thief.'

'So why do they think that you are a thief now?' I asked.

'Because some of the jewellery was in the **parcel** I took to Dubai,' he smiled at our surprised faces, but it wasn't a happy smile.

'Of course I didn't know what was in the parcel. The parcel was on my desk at work the evening before I went to Dubai. There was a **typed** note from Sheikh Bin Salem's secretary. Well, I thought that it was from his secretary. The note asked me to take the parcel to Dubai the next morning. I didn't open the parcel. I never do. The note said that there were important papers for Sheikh Bin Salem's family inside the parcel. I have taken important papers for him many times before. He trusts me more than anyone – or he did,' he said sadly.

'Did you show the note to the police?' I asked.

'Of course, but the secretary said that he didn't type the note

parcel a paper box with things in

type to write on a computer or typewriter

and Sheikh Bin Salem said that he didn't ask the secretary to type it.'

'Who do you think typed it, father?' asked Mohammed, my twelve-year-old brother.

'I don't know. The police think that I typed it myself.'

'Where did you take the parcel?' asked Amira.

'The note asked me to take it to an address in Dubai, to the brother of Sheikh Bin Salem's wife in Dubai. When I got there, I went into the house. I met a tall man there. I thought that he was the brother. We drank coffee. We talked for a few minutes and I gave him the parcel. Then I left.'

'Wasn't he her brother?' asked Ibrahim.

'No. Later, much later, the police told me that he buys and sells stolen jewellery. They were already watching him. Then they saw me arrive, get out of the car with the parcel and go

'I thought that he was the brother.'

15

into his house. When I left, they **arrested** me, the driver, and the tall man.'

'What did the tall man say?' I asked.

'He said that someone phoned him. A man told him that he was bringing some expensive jewellery to his house. He didn't know the man's name. Perhaps it was me or perhaps it was another man. He wasn't sure.'

'What happened at the police station?' Ibrahim asked.

'They put me in a room and left me. Nobody spoke to me. Nobody told me anything. Then, after about two hours, a policeman came into the room, an important policeman. I told him that there was a mistake, but he just laughed. I explained that it wasn't my parcel. I was just taking it to that address. He became angry. He started shouting. He told me that I would stay at the police station until he heard the **truth**.'

'Were you afraid?' asked Mohammed.

My father smiled. 'No, but I was worried about you. You were waiting for me to come home.'

'What happened next, father?' asked Amira.

'Another policeman came into the room about two hours later. He took me to an office, the office of the important policeman. He asked me more questions. He knew everything about me – my job, my address, your schools and university, he even knew about your engagement, Kareem!'

'But there has been no announcement yet!' I said.

'I know. He had a lot of information.' He looked at my mother and I. 'Have you spoken to Samira and her family yet?'

'Her mother phoned two days ago. She was worried about you. I told her that you would be home soon and that everything would be fine. I haven't spoken to her since then,' my mother said.

'I spoke to Samira yesterday. She told me that it must be a mistake. She said that nobody would **believe** it,' I said.

arrest to take a person to prison

truth something that is true

believe to feel sure something is true

'She's a nice girl, but still young. She doesn't know people very well,' my father said.

'Go on with the story, father,' said Mohammed.

'You know the rest of the story. Your uncle came to the police station and phoned Sheikh Bin Salem. The police wanted to send me to prison for taking the jewels but Sheikh Bin Salem was against it. I've worked for him for a long time. He said to the police that perhaps my story was true. In the end, the police said that I could leave.'

'What are you going to do now?' asked Ibrahim.

'I want to forget these last few days. I want to go back to work. I want to do what I usually do, but I don't think that I can. Sheikh Bin Salem told me to take a long holiday. He wants to give people time. He wants to give them time to forget all this. I don't think that they will forget it, but Sheikh Bin Salem has been very good to me so I must agree to his plans.'

'But there has been no announcement!'

'One day the police will catch the real thief and then we can forget all about this,' said my mother.

'Now please children, leave me alone. I'm feeling very tired,' said my father.

We all left the room. Catch the real thief! Were the police even looking? I turned around and opened the door again. My father was sitting on the chair. His head was in his hands.

READING CHECK

Match the first and second parts of these sentences.

a Back at home Kareem's father . . . ☐3

b Two weeks before the drive to Dubai someone . . . ☐

c Some of the stolen jewellery . . . ☐

d A note told Kareem's father . . . ☐

e In Dubai, Kareem's father . . . ☐

f At the police station Kareem's father . . . ☐

g The important policeman in Dubai . . . ☐

h Sheikh Bin Salem . . . ☐

1 had stolen some jewellery from Sheikh Bin Salem's house.

2 to take the parcel to the brother of Sheikh Bin Salem's wife in Dubai.

3 tells his children that he isn't a thief.

4 met a tall man who buys stolen jewellery.

5 wants Kareem's father to take a long holiday from work.

6 was in the parcel that Kareem's father took to Dubai.

7 tells an important policeman that the parcel wasn't his.

8 knows about Kareem's and Samira's engagement.

WORD WORK

Use the words from the puzzle to complete the sentences on page 19.

a Sheikh Bin Salem is Kareem's father's . . . . *boss* . . . .

b I don't want you to write that letter by hand. Can you . . . . it?

c Kareem's father found a parcel and a . . . . note on his desk one evening.

d Kareem's father must take the . . . . to a man in Dubai.

e In Dubai the police . . . . Kareem's father for selling stolen jewellery.

f An important policemen in Dubai tells Kareem's father that he wants to hear the . . . . from him.

g Samira says people won't . . . . that Kareem's father is a thief.

GUESS WHAT

What happens in the next chapter? Tick four sentences.

a ☐ Samira's father says 'no' to Samira's engagement with Kareem.

b ☐ Lots of people come to visit Kareem's father at home.

c ☐ Nobody comes to visit Kareem's home.

d ☐ Kareem's father goes back to work.

e ☐ Samira phones Kareem.

f ☐ Kareem decides to find the real jewellery thief.

CHAPTER 4
A quiet house

Life was bad. The next day it was worse. Samira's father phoned. He wanted to speak to my father. I looked at my father while he took the call. After a minute or two he put his hand over the phone and turned to me. He asked me to leave the room. Ten minutes later, he called me back and told me the bad news.

'I'm very sorry, my son. When they arrested me, I thought about your engagement. I was afraid of this. Samira's father has just phoned. He said that his plans have changed. He said that he thinks Samira is too young. I'm so sorry. I've done nothing wrong and neither have you, but that's not important now.'

'Samira's father knows that you're a good man. How can he do this to you, to our family? It's not right,' I said angrily.

'We know that I'm not a thief and I think that he knows that, too. But he's thinking about his daughter. How can he agree to this engagement now? Nobody wants to know a thief – or the family of a thief. He doesn't want his daughter to marry into a family that nobody wants to know. You'll see. He won't be the only one to think that way.'

My father was right. We usually had a lot of visitors: my mother's family and friends, our friends, my father's family, friends and business **colleagues**. There was always someone in the house. Now the house was empty. Nobody came to visit. Nobody came for dinner or for coffee. I spoke to my friends on the phone, but, strangely, they were always busy. Amira and Ibrahim said the same. Luckily it was the summer. There was no school for my youngest brother. We were happy about that. We didn't want him to hear bad things about his father from the other children. But Mohammed wasn't happy. He was bored. He didn't have anyone to play with. He stayed

colleague
someone that
you work with

in his bedroom and played on his computer. He only left his room to eat and to tell us that he was bored.

We didn't see much of my father either. He lived in his own world. Day after day, he sat in his office, seeing nobody, talking to nobody. He stopped eating with us, so my mother took food to him. He ate very little. My mother didn't say anything to me, but I knew that she was very worried about him and the family. Sometimes at night, when she thought that we were all in bed, I could hear her downstairs, crying.

Not everyone stopped calling. The day after Samira's father phoned, I had a phone call from Samira.

'I'm so sorry,' she said. She was crying. 'I don't want to end our engagement, but my father won't listen. I told my father that there has been a terrible mistake. I know that your father isn't a thief and I'm sure that my father knows that too, but he says it's not important what he or I think. He told me that he spoke to your father.'

'Yes, he did,' I said quietly.

'One day the police will catch the real thief and everyone will be sorry,' she said.

'I'll never forget your trust in my family,' I said quietly. 'Thank you.'

'Perhaps we can help my father change his plans again,' she went on, and she wasn't crying now. 'We must find the real thief. Your father didn't take the jewellery, so we must find the person who did.' She made it sound so easy.

'But how are we going to do that?' I asked.

'Let's think. Sheikh Bin Salem says that he didn't leave the parcel. He says that he didn't ask his secretary to type it. Perhaps he didn't ask him to type it, but perhaps he left the parcel.'

'What do you mean?' I asked.

'Perhaps he typed the note himself. Perhaps *he* stole his wife's jewellery.'

I was **shocked** at her words. 'I know you want to help my father, but Sheikh Bin Salem isn't a thief,' I said.

'Why not? He can sell the jewellery and get money from the **insurance company** at the same time. Then he can buy his wife new jewellery and have the rest of the money for himself.'

'He doesn't need to do that. He's a very rich man.'

'Sheikh Bin Salem isn't a thief.'

'Perhaps he is, perhaps he isn't. How do we know? Perhaps he has money problems. Perhaps he just thinks it is exciting to be a thief. I don't know why he did it, but we have to find out more about him – and everyone who went into your father's office on that day,' she said.

I didn't think she was right about Sheikh Bin Salem, but I wanted to do something. So I agreed.

'OK. Let's try,' I said. 'The first thing I can do is to talk to Abu Malek. He makes the coffee and tea at the Eastern Trading Company. He sees everybody who goes in and out of the building. Perhaps he can remember who came in and out of the building that day.'

'Good. When you get the information, phone me. I'm sure that we can find the real thief,' she said.

shocked to feel surprised about something bad

insurance company you pay money to this business and it pays you when something bad happens

The next day I went early to the Eastern Trading Company to speak to Abu Malek. I waited outside the building. About ten minutes later I saw him, walking down the street. He was angry about what people were saying, he told me. He liked my father.

'People say that he's a thief. They're wrong. Your father's

a good man. When my wife was sick, he helped me. He gave me money to buy her what she needed. He's a kind man.'

'Thank you,' I said. 'My father needs help now. He travelled to Dubai last Friday. I need to know what happened the day before he went. Who went to my father's office? Can you remember?' I asked.

'Let me think for a while,' he said. 'Last Thursday . . .' he thought for a moment. 'Yes, now I remember . . . I went into your father's office four or five times to take him a cup of coffee. I do that every day. His colleague Mr Nasser came in while I was there. He doesn't drink coffee in the mornings. He prefers tea.'

'What time was this?' I asked.

'I think it was about ten o'clock. He was in the office for about an hour I think. He left, and about five minutes later, Mr Moussa went in. I took them both coffee. He was in there for about half an hour. Your father left for lunch around two o'clock as usual. All the other employees left then too. Your father came back about four o'clock. Oh yes, he had two visitors in the afternoon. They arrived just after your father. I took them coffee. I don't know who they were, but they were from Jordan. They stayed for about an hour.'

'Why not?'

'Were there any other visitors?' I asked.

'No, only Sheikh Bin Salem, but he's not a visitor! He came to the office in the evening. He usually comes around six or seven o'clock. He spoke to your father, but he didn't go to your father's office.

23

Your father always goes to Sheikh Bin Salem's office. Your father was carrying a lot of papers with him. I took them coffee and then closed the door. It was a long meeting. About two hours later your father opened the door and asked me to bring two cups of coffee. They were laughing about something.'

'Who left the building first, Sheikh Bin Salem or my father?' I asked.

'Sheikh Bin Salem. I think he left about half past eight. All the other employees left between eight and nine o'clock. After nine, the only people in the building were your father and I . . . oh yes, the cleaners were there, too, and the **security guard** was outside as usual.'

'What time did my father leave?' I asked.

'Wait, now I remember. The son of Sheikh Bin Salem. He was here, too. He arrived just after nine. He was looking for his father. I told him that Sheikh Bin Salem wasn't here. He asked me for coffee. I made it and took it to his father's office. He left about ten minutes later.'

'Did he go to my father's office?'

'I didn't see him go in. No, he didn't. I saw your father later. He didn't know about Omar's visit. He was surprised. We don't usually see Omar. His father wanted him to work here, but Omar has his own business. His father was angry, but Omar has never listened to his father or anyone. Omar likes to do things his way.'

I thanked Abu Malek for his help and left the building.

As soon as I got into my car, I phoned Samira and told her everything.

'It can't be Mr Nasser or Mr Moussa or any of the other employees,' she said. 'Your father said that he found the parcel just before he left. So there are only four **suspects** on our **list** – Sheikh Bin Salem, his son, Abu Malek, or the cleaners.'

I was shocked. 'Samira,' I said, 'I think that you are wrong about Sheikh Bin Salem. The thief's not him or his son. And

security guard
someone who watches a building and stops thieves from going in

suspect you think that this person has done something wrong but you are not sure

list a lot of names that you write one after the other

24

Abu Malek's a very **honest** man. Perhaps the cleaners did it or someone that Abu Malek didn't see.'

'Perhaps you're right, but let's begin with our four suspects. I must go now. We have visitors. Let's think about what we're going to do next. I'll call you tomorrow,' she said.

honest someone who doesn't steal

'Wait, now I remember.'

25

READING CHECK

Correct eight more mistakes in the chapter summary.

Samira's father phones Kareem's father and says that Samira is too ~~old~~ *young* to

marry. Suddenly everybody comes to visit Kareem's house. Kareem's father

stays in his bed and eats very little. Kareem's mother laughs at night when she

thinks her children are in bed. The day after her father phones, Samira writes to

Kareem. She is interested in finding who took Sheikh Bin Salem's jewellery. The

next week Kareem goes to speak to Abu Malek. He makes the lunch and dinner

at the Eastern Trading Company. Later Kareem talks to his mother on the phone

and they decide that the only names on their list of people who perhaps took the

jewellery are Sheikh Bin Salem, his son Omar, Abu Malek, and the cleaners.

WORD WORK

Match the words in the office buildings with the underlined words in the sentences.

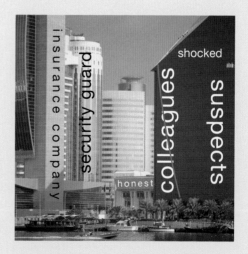

a Mr Nasser and Mr Moussa are <u>people who work together</u> at the Eastern Trading Company.

......*colleagues*......

b Kareem is <u>very surprised</u> when Samira says that perhaps Sheikh Bin Salem stole his wife's jewellery.

....

c Abu Malek is <u>not a person who steals things</u>. . . . .

d Sheikh Bin Salem, Omar, Abu Malek, and the cleaners are all <u>people who perhaps did something wrong</u> on Kareem's and Samira's list. . . . .

e There is a <u>person who watches people going in and out</u> outside the Eastern Trading Company Building. . . . .

f Perhaps Sheikh Bin Salem wanted money from his <u>company that gives you money when something bad happens to you</u>. . . . .

GUESS WHAT

What happens in the next chapter? Tick the boxes.

a Samira . . .

   1 ☐ catches the thief.

   2 ☐ phones Kareem.

   3 ☐ marries another man.

b Kareem questions . . .

   1 ☐ Sheikh Bin Salem, the owner of the Eastern Trading Company.

   2 ☐ Sheikh Bin Salem's son, Omar.

   3 ☐ his own father.

c Last year Sheikh Bin Salem gave . . .

   1 ☐ his son Omar lots of money to start an Internet business.

   2 ☐ his son Omar a job in the Eastern Trading Company.

   3 ☐ nothing to his son Omar.

d Kareem and Samira think that the person who took the jewellery was . . .

   1 ☐ one of Sheikh Bin Salem's maids.

   2 ☐ one of the office cleaners at the Eastern Trading Company.

   3 ☐ Sheikh Bin Salem's son Omar.

CHAPTER 5

More questions

I was having breakfast when my phone rang. It was Samira. I left the room. I didn't want the rest of my family to hear me.

'I've thought about this all night. I think that you're right about Abu Malek. Perhaps he put the parcel on your father's desk, but how could he get the jewellery from Sheikh Bin Salem's house? What about the cleaners? Perhaps they work in Sheikh Bin Salem's company and in his house, too. Perhaps they stole the jewellery and put it on your father's desk. We must find out.'

'Okay, that's easy. I'll ask my father.'

'And we must find out if Sheikh Bin Salem or his son needs money. You can ask your father about Sheikh Bin Salem's business. I can ask my father about Omar. My father knows everybody who works in the **Internet** business.'

'Even if we know who did it, I don't know how we can **prove** it to the police,' I said.

'I don't know how we'll do it, but we must try,' said Samira.

That evening I knocked on the door of my father's office and went in. My father was sitting behind his desk, looking out of the window. He looked very sad.

'Father, I must speak to you. Who cleans your office?'

'What a strange question! Why do you want to know?'

'We know that you didn't take the jewellery. Perhaps the cleaners took it from Sheikh Bin Salem's house and brought it to the office.'

'We have two men from Pakistan to clean the office. They've been working there for about three years. I think that they're honest. They've never taken anything before – not even a pencil. They don't clean Sheikh Bin Salem's house. He has two **maids** from the Philippines at home. They're sisters and

Internet using computers

prove to show that something is certainly true

maid a woman who cleans and tidies a house

they have worked for him for many years. Of course, the police have been into their room and looked through all their things carefully, but they found nothing.'

'I have another question. Do you think Sheikh Bin Salem needs money? Is the Eastern Trading Company doing well?'

'Last year was difficult for the company, but not this year. Last year we bought a lot of new computers and we opened a new office in Dubai. It was an expensive year for Sheikh Bin Salem. His son Omar started his Internet business, and he had to give him a lot of money. But this year is very good. We've got a lot of business and I think we'll get more. It'll be a good year for the company.'

'What about Omar? How is his business doing?'

'I'm not sure. I asked Sheikh Bin Salem about it a few weeks ago, but he told me not to ask him. He said that he didn't want to talk about Omar or what he's doing. He looked angry. You know that Sheikh Bin Salem wanted Omar to work with

My father spoke to Sheikh Bin Salem a few weeks ago.

argument an
angry talk

throw away (*past*
threw, thrown) to
put something into
the rubbish

him, but Omar wanted to set up this Internet business. They
had many **arguments**, but Sheikh Bin Salem gave him the
money in the end.'

'Interesting,' I said.

'Omar doesn't always listen to his parents, but that doesn't
mean he stole from them. He comes from a good family. He's
not a thief.'

I didn't say anything, but suddenly I wasn't so sure any
more. After I left the room I phoned Samira.

'I think that we can take the cleaners off our list of suspects
for now,' she agreed. 'Like Abu Malek, it's easy for them to go
into your father's office, but difficult for them to get the jewellery.
I've got interesting news about Omar, too. My father says that
there are a lot of companies in the Internet business now. It's
not like before. And Omar's spending a lot of money. My father
thinks that Omar's spending more than he's making.'

'So Omar stays on our list. But if he's the thief, how can we
prove it?' I asked.

'Let's think. The police said that not all the jewellery was
in the parcel. They're still looking for the rest of it. If Omar's
the thief, the jewellery must be with him – in his house or
car or office. We must find it. Then we
can prove that he's the thief and not
your father.'

'The police?'

'It could be anywhere.
Perhaps he's **thrown** it
away,' I said.

'I don't think so. He
still needs money. And
I don't think that he's
worried about your
father or the police.
Remember he stole
from his parents.'

'Well, we're not sure about that,' I said.

Samira wasn't listening. 'I don't think that it's in his house,' she went on. 'It's too dangerous. Someone might find it. Perhaps he took it to his office.'

'It's a good place to begin. I must get into his office and look around,' I said.

'How are you going to do that?'

'I can go in the evening after all the employees have left. Who goes into offices and companies in the evening without problems?' I asked.

'The police?'

'Cleaners! Perhaps I can **disguise** myself as a cleaner and get into his office. But I don't want the real cleaners to be there.'

'I know!' said Samira. 'My sister wants some men to work in her garden. She wants to build a small house for the children. I'll send my driver to find the cleaners. I'll pay them a lot of money, but they must work in the evening. We'll tell them that we don't want the children to see the house until it's ready.'

Later that day she phoned me again.

'My driver found the cleaners. Everything is OK for tomorrow.'

'Wonderful. I think I'll ask my brother Ibrahim to come with me. We can borrow the cleaners' clothes and carry **buckets** and some **mops**. I'm sure that nobody will look at us.'

disguise to pretend to be someone else

bucket you can carry water in this

mop a long brush for washing the floor

'Cleaners!'

31

READING CHECK

Match the sentences with the people.

a ☐4 agrees with Kareem that Abu Malek didn't take the jewellery.

b ☐ doesn't listen to his parents.

c ☐ has maids from the Philippines at home.

d ☐ has Pakistani office cleaners.

e ☐ needed money last year to start a business.

f ☐ has interesting news about Omar.

g ☐ is spending lots of money.

h ☐ decides to visit the Eastern Trading Company at night.

1 KAREEM

2 OMAR

3 SHEIKH BIN SALEM

4 SAMIRA

WORD WORK

Find words in the necklace to complete the sentences on page 33.

a Sheikh Bin Salem's . . . . *maids* . . . . are sisters.

b Omar has an . . . . business.

c Omar and Sheikh Bin Salem had an . . . . when Omar decided not to work in his father's company.

d Kareem and Samira keep Omar on their . . . . of suspects.

e Kareem wants to find who took the jewellery and to . . . . that they are the thief.

f Kareem decides to get into Omar's Internet business building in a cleaner's . . . .

g You use a . . . . to clean floors.

h You carry water in a . . . .

i Samira doesn't think the thief has . . . . the rest of the Sheikh's jewellery.

GUESS WHAT

What happens in the next chapter? Match the parts of the sentences.

a Kareem and Ibrahim go together . . .

1 but they say nothing.

b They find a fat man . . .

2 as cleaners into Omar's office building.

c The security guard speaks to them . . .

3 when he gets home.

d Kareem wants to film Omar . . .

4 with the stolen jewellery.

e Kareem phones Samira . . .

5 working late in one of the offices.

CHAPTER 6

Buckets and mops

Later that evening my brother and I arrived at Omar's company. The big, glass door at the front of the building was open. A security guard was standing outside. He was talking to another man. We walked past with our heads down. We were disguised as cleaners and carried brushes and mops which we held near our faces, but I was afraid. This was dangerous. We could be in big trouble for this. But there was no other way to help our father.

The guard didn't look at us. He was too busy, talking to his friend. We were in the building. There were two floors. The ground floor was one long room with a bathroom and a kitchen at the end. There were a lot of desks and computers in the long room. How could Omar hide the jewellery here? Too many people. He probably had an office upstairs. But first we had to look around here.

I opened a big cupboard. Nothing interesting there. I opened a second cupboard and stopped. There was a noise. I looked at my brother. He was looking at a man, a very fat man, working at a computer in the corner of the room. I looked at my brother again. He was thinking the same as me. What are we going to do? Shall we run away? Shall we get out of the building before it's too late? I shook my head. No. It was going to be more difficult and dangerous than we thought, but we must try.

Please let this man be very busy, I **prayed**. Just then, the phone rang and the man began talking on the phone.

'What shall I do?' asked Ibrahim quietly.

'Go and bring some water from the kitchen. We'll begin washing the floor over here,' I said.

Ibrahim washed the floor and I cleaned the desks. While I was cleaning the desks, I looked in the **drawers**. Again nothing. But what about the man's desk? I didn't want to go near him,

pray to talk to God

drawer a thing like a box which you can pull out from a desk or other piece of furniture

but perhaps he wanted me to clean it. I didn't know what to do. Then the man spoke.

cough to make a noise in your throat

'I'll be finished in five minutes and then you can clean my desk.'

A few minutes later the fat man stood up.

'You can clean it now,' he said and walked to the kitchen.

I quickly cleaned his desk. Ibrahim was watching the kitchen. There were two drawers in the desk. I opened the first one. Just some pens and an address book. I opened the second. There was a white box. I put my hand into the drawer and touched the box. Ibrahim **coughed**. I quickly pulled my hand out of the drawer and closed it. The fat man was coming back. I turned away and began cleaning another desk. Then the phone rang and the man sat down again.

Ibrahim and I went into the kitchen.

'Remember we don't have to clean everything. Just clean what people will see,' I said. But it was hard work. My brother and I never cleaned at home.

'It's going to be a long evening,' he said quietly.

Half an hour later we were finished and ready to go upstairs. We had to walk through the long room again. This time the fat man wasn't there. I went to his desk again. Ibrahim was watching for the man. I opened the drawer and looked in the

'You can clean it now.'

box. It was only a **computer mouse**. I closed the drawer and we walked towards the stairs. Where was the fat man?

Then we saw him. He was at the front door, talking to the guard. We walked upstairs with our buckets and mops and pushed open the glass doors. There were doors to four offices, and to a bathroom and a kitchen. The first and biggest office was Omar's. His name was on the door.

'If we don't find the jewellery here, I don't know what we'll do,' I said.

'Well, this is the best place to begin,' said Ibrahim.

Inside the office was a black **sofa**, two comfortable chairs, and a glass table. There were two large, green **plants** next to the door. Behind the sofa there was a large cupboard with books inside. Across the room was a big desk and a black chair. Everything looked very expensive. There were windows on two sides of the room. You could see the beach and the sea from them. On the left was a small bathroom.

'We must be very careful. If you move anything, put it back in the same place,' I said. 'I'll look behind the desk. You look in the cupboard.'

I opened each drawer in the desk, one by one. In the third drawer I saw a blue box. My hands were **sweating**. Was it a jewellery box? I took the box out of the drawer and called Ibrahim. He stood next to me as I opened the box. But no. Inside was just an expensive pen with the name of the company in gold on its side. I put it back.

'Nothing in the cupboard,' said my brother.

I pulled the **handle** of the last drawer. It didn't open.

'Omar has **locked** this. Why? What's he hiding inside?'

'Let's break the lock,' replied my brother.

'Wait a minute. If we take the jewellery with us, the police will say that we got it from our father. And if the jewellery isn't here, we'll still be in trouble. Omar will see the broken lock and he'll know that someone was looking in his office.'

computer mouse this helps you work on the computer

sofa a long soft seat for people to sit on together

plant a green thing like a small tree

sweat to get water on your body because you are hot or worried

handle you move this to open a door or pull out a drawer

lock to close with a key

'So what are we going to do?' asked Ibrahim.

'I don't know. But let's look in the other offices first. Perhaps it's not here. Perhaps we'll find the jewellery in another room.'

We opened all the other drawers and cupboards, but we found nothing interesting. We went back to Omar's office.

'This is the only locked drawer in the building. It must be in here,' said Ibrahim.

'Of course. His office is the best place to hide the jewellery. Employees don't look in these drawers,' I said.

I thought for a moment, and then it came to me. 'We need to photograph him, opening the drawer and holding the jewellery. Then we could prove that he's the thief,' I said.

'Well, there's nowhere to hide in this room,' said my brother.

I walked over to the window. 'We must help our father. We must find a way,' I thought. I looked out of the window. There was a small **balcony** outside.

'That's it!' I said. 'I know what I can do.'

I told Ibrahim my plan. I could photograph Omar from outside. I could wait on the balcony for him.

'Or you could film him. He'll see the **flash** from a camera. A video camera is better than a camera. Uncle Ahmed has a very good video camera. We could borrow it,' he said.

'But I can't wait here for days and days. He must open the drawer while I'm watching from the balcony. But how can I make him open it?'

'We don't have time to think about that now,' said Ibrahim. 'Let's go and find the door to the balcony.'

We left the room and immediately we saw the door to the balcony. We unlocked it and walked along the balcony towards Omar's office.

'I can **kneel** here and hold the video camera up. From here I can film the desk, the drawer and the jewellery,' I said.

'If the jewellery is here! Now let's finish this cleaning and get out of the building,' said Ibrahim.

balcony a place where you can sit or stand, outside a building and above the ground

flash a bright light

kneel to rest on your knees

He'll know that I'm not from Pakistan, I thought.

We walked down the stairs. The security guard was near the front door. Was he waiting for us? I turned my face down towards the floor. My brush and mop were in front of my face.

'You took a long time tonight. Bring your old buckets and mops tomorrow,' he laughed. 'Not these new ones.'

If I speak, he'll know that I'm not from Pakistan, I thought. If I don't speak, he'll think that something is wrong. Then help arrived. A car stopped in front of the building. The driver wanted to speak to the security guard. The guard walked over to the car and we hurried away.

I was happy to see my car. We got in. I looked at my watch.

'We weren't long. Not bad for beginners,' I said, smiling.

'My back hurts and I'm tired,' said Ibrahim.

'It's not an easy job. Perhaps you'll be tidier at home now.'

'Are you my mother or my brother?'

When we got home I went to my room. I wanted to phone Samira and tell her the news.

'I'm sure that you're right,' she said. 'If it's the only locked drawer in the building, the jewellery must be inside it. But how can you make Omar open the drawer?'

'Why don't I call the police?'

'They won't believe you.'

'Perhaps I should start a fire?' I **joked**.

'Too dangerous. I know. I'll phone him. I'll tell him that I know that he is the thief. I'll tell him that I have the jewellery now. I'll ask him for 10,000 dollars or I'll speak to the police. Of course, he'll immediately go to his office and open that drawer. He'll want to see if the jewellery is there or not. You'll be on the balcony, waiting for him. If you film him, we can prove that he's the thief and not your father.'

'I can only go to his company at night. I can't hide on the balcony in the day. The other employees will see me.'

'You can clean the office again on Thursday evening. Stay there all night. I'll phone Omar on Friday morning. Nobody works on Friday.'

'If two cleaners go into the building and only one leaves, the security guard will look for me.'

'Can you climb up to the first floor from the outside of the building?' she asked.

'No. But I can open a small window in the bathroom on the ground floor. I can climb up to that. Of course if someone is working late, it will be difficult to get to the first floor.'

'You must climb in very late at night – and pray that everyone is asleep,' she said.

joke to say something funny

READING CHECK

Complete the sentences with the correct names.

a Kareem and ☐ Samira ☑ Ibrahim go to work as cleaners.

b They go to clean ☐ Sheikh Bin Salem's ☐ Omar's building.

c They find ☐ a fat man ☐ Omar in the office.

d They decide to borrow a video camera from ☐ Uncle Ahmed. ☐ Samira's father.

e ☐ The security guard ☐ Omar tells them to bring their old mops the next day.

f ☐ Kareem ☐ Kareem's father tells Ibrahim that perhaps after cleaning offices he'll be tidier at home.

g ☐ Ibrahim ☐ Samira tells Kareem to go back to the office on Thursday night.

WORD WORK

1 Correct the underlined words in the sentences.

a There is a large black <u>soft</u> in Omar's office. .... *sofa* ....

b There are two green <u>planes</u> by the door. ....

c Kareem pulls a <u>candle</u> on Omar's desk but he can't open it. ....

d He's excited and his hands start to <u>sweet</u>. ....

e Ibrahim <u>toughs</u> to tell his brother to be careful because someone is coming.

....

f Kareem <u>plays</u> that the fat man in the office will be too busy to talk to them.

....

2 Find seven more words from Chapter 6 in the wordsquare and match them with the definitions.

a ....locked....... closed with a key

b .... not working

c .... not closed with a key

d .... an open place on the side of a building

e .... to get down on your knees

f .... to say something to make people laugh

g .... you hold this in your hand to make a computer work

h .... you put things away in this; it is in the front of a desk

p	l	b	r	o	k	e	n
c	o	m	p	u	t	e	r
j	c	m	m	o	u	s	e
o	k	n	e	e	l	s	t
k	e	n	b	g	l	s	t
e	d	r	a	w	e	r	t
u	b	a	l	c	o	n	y
u	n	l	o	c	k	e	d

GUESS WHAT

What happens in the next chapter? Write *Kareem*, *Ibrahim*, *Samira*, or *Omar* in each sentence.

a .... films Omar.

b .... helps Kareem through the bathroom window.

c .... takes a pen from his desk.

d .... phones Omar.

e .... sends a text message to Kareem.

f .... is afraid the police are coming for him.

g .... gets the stolen necklace.

41

CHAPTER 7

A big day

On Thursday morning Samira phoned me again.

'Everything's OK. The cleaners will go back to my sister's place to paint the children's house. I had to pay them more. They're worried about losing their cleaning jobs.'

'I think Ibrahim and I did a very good cleaning job last night!' I joked. 'But after tonight I don't ever want to do it again.

'That evening Ibrahim and I went back to Omar's company. Before I left my house I took some food for the next day's breakfast. I put the bread and cheese in my bucket. Ibrahim had the video camera in his bucket. This time we went to Omar's office first. I looked at my watch. It took four minutes from the front door to the office.

As soon as I arrived in Omar's office I went to his desk. The drawer was still locked.

'OK, you stay here, behind the desk,' I said to Ibrahim, 'I'm going to try filming from the balcony.'

I went outside and kneeled down below the window. I held the video camera up above my head and began filming Ibrahim. The first time I got the desk and his arm, but not his face. The next time I got his face, but not the drawer. I filmed him five or six times before it was right. I took a pencil from one of the desks and **drew** a line on the wall under the window. Tomorrow morning I'll kneel here, I thought to myself.

I heard a noise. It was Ibrahim. He was knocking on the glass. Someone was coming. I ran along the balcony and through the door. Ibrahim was in front of me. He gave me a mop and we both began cleaning the floor. I looked up, carefully. It was Omar.

draw (*past* **drew**) to make a picture with a pen or pencil

He was going into his office. Ibrahim and I looked at each other. All this hard work for nothing! A few minutes later

Omar came out again. He had something in his hand. He went out of the glass doors and downstairs. We walked quickly to his office, to his desk. The drawer was still locked. But was it now empty? I opened the first drawer. Everything was there. I opened the second and then the third. The blue box wasn't there in the third drawer. I wanted to laugh.

The first time I got the desk and his arm.

'It's OK, Ibrahim. He took the pen. Perhaps he wants to give someone a present.'

I went back to the balcony for the video camera. We hid it in a cupboard in the kitchen.

'Now for the cleaning,' I said to Ibrahim.

'Do we have to do it? We're not coming back,' he said.

'We don't know what will happen tomorrow,' I told him. 'Perhaps Omar won't come. Perhaps his phone's not working. Something could go wrong. Perhaps we'll need to come back, so let's do the cleaning tonight.'

We went downstairs. The fat man from the night before was there again. He was talking on the phone. We worked very quickly this time. When we got near the man, he stood up and told us to clean his desk. When we finished, I went into the bathroom. I opened a small window in the corner of the room. I didn't want the fat man or the guard to see the unlocked window so I took the **light bulb** out of the bathroom light. I was pleased with myself. It will be difficult to see the window because now it's dark in the bathroom, I thought.

We were now ready to leave. We walked to the front door. The security guard was sitting next to the door, drinking coffee and talking to a friend. He didn't look at us. We hurried down the street and round the corner. There we got into the car and drove away. I drove to a quiet place and Ibrahim and I changed out of our cleaning clothes and changed into our usual clothes.

Hours later, we left our house again. It was two o'clock in the morning. Everywhere was quiet. We drove near Omar's office building, stopped the car, got out and walked around the back of the building. I put my foot in my brother's hands and he pushed me up. Finally I could pull myself up and through the window. I was back inside!

The bathroom door was open. There was a light outside but no noise. I decided to **crawl**. I came out of the bathroom on my hands and **knees**. The fat man wasn't at his desk, but his computer was on. I crawled some more and saw a man's foot on the floor. He was asleep on the carpet. A few minutes later I was at the glass doors next to the stairs. The front door of the building wasn't open and there was no light on the stairs. It was very dark. I walked upstairs, slowly and carefully.

light bulb this is made from glass and it gives light

crawl to move along slowly with your body near the floor

knee the place which moves in the middle of your leg

I went to Omar's office first. The drawer was still locked. I came out of his room and went into another room, near Omar's office and the balcony door. There was a large desk in the office. I moved the chair back and crawled under the table. I made myself as comfortable as possible, closed my eyes and tried to sleep.

Two hours later I woke up. It was still dark. I heard **footsteps** outside and saw a light. The security guard had a **torch** and he was walking around outside the office. The footsteps were coming nearer. The door of the office opened and he **shone** his torch into the room. If he finds me, I'll be in a lot of trouble with the police and my parents, I thought. Big trouble. The guard shone the light around the room and then back to the desk. I didn't move. Then the light moved away again and the door closed. I looked at my watch. It was five o'clock in the morning. I waited for half an hour and then crawled out. My back hurt. I felt terrible. I don't want to do this again, I thought.

I walked quietly towards the stairs. It was dark downstairs. I was sure that the guard was asleep again. I went to the bathroom and put cold water on my face to wake myself up. Then I went to the kitchen, drank a cup of water, and ate some bread and cheese. It was still early. I got the video camera and opened the balcony door. I sat down under the window and waited. I looked at my watch again and again. Samira is going to phone Omar in thirty minutes. She's going to phone him in twenty minutes, in ten minutes, in five. I was counting the minutes. Then I got a text message from Samira. It said only one word 'OK'. Thank you, Samira, I thought, I won't forget your help.

Now for the second text message. Ibrahim was waiting outside the building. He was waiting for Omar to arrive. About half an hour later I got a text message from Ibrahim. Omar was here. Now I must do my job, I said to myself. Samira and Ibrahim have done their jobs very well. And you must do the same.

footsteps the noise people make with their feet when they walk

torch a light that you can carry with you

shine (*past* **shone**) to put the light of a torch on something

I was ready. I held the video camera up and started filming. Carefully I moved my head up. I wanted to look. The long minutes passed. But where was Omar? He wasn't at his desk. He wasn't in the room. Perhaps he was in the bathroom, but the office door was still closed. Was he still walking up the stairs? I couldn't hear any footsteps. Where was he?

What did he want to put in there?

I knew then that we were wrong. We were wrong about the drawer. We were so sure, but so wrong. But why was Omar here? Perhaps the jewellery was in the building, but not in his office, in another place. I had to follow him. I ran back along the balcony and then stopped, suddenly. There he was. Omar was standing near the door of another office. He was playing with a plant. What was he doing? How strange! He had a spoon in his hand and he was making a hole with it in the **soil** around the plant. What did he want to put in there? No, stupid, I said to myself. He isn't putting something in. He's taking something out. And yes, a minute or two later, he pulled out a bag. He opened it and pulled out a beautiful diamond necklace. The stolen jewellery!

And I wasn't filming. I was so busy, watching Omar, I forgot to film him. I quickly began filming, but it was too late. Omar was walking away, the bag in his hand. It was a **disaster**! What could I say to Samira and Ibrahim? And my father? How could I help him now?

But wait, I thought, perhaps I can still film him. I'm sure Omar's hands are dirty now from the soil. Perhaps he'll wash them in the bathroom in his office. I ran as fast as I could to Omar's office. I got on my knees and looked inside the room. At last, I had some good luck. The jewellery was on his desk, the necklace and the earrings. I began filming. The door to the bathroom was open, but I couldn't see Omar through it. Was he inside? I had to film him with the jewellery. If I don't film him, he will say that I put the jewellery on his desk.

And then I heard a police car. It was coming nearer. I held the video camera up, but my hands were sweating. Perhaps Omar could see me. Perhaps the police were coming for me. Omar will say that I am stealing from his company, I thought. A thief like his father. The car was very close now. What am I going to do? How can I explain? Will the police believe me, or Omar? But then the noise went away. I smiled to myself. It was stupid to be afraid. They weren't coming for me. Not now. But the film? Was Omar in it – with the jewellery?

soil trees and plants live in this

disaster a very bad thing

READING CHECK

Correct the mistakes in these sentences.

Kareem

a ~~Ibrahim~~ tries to film Omar's office from the balcony.

b Sheikh Bin Salem visits his office when Kareem and Ibrahim are in the building.

c Kareem stops the door working in the bathroom on the ground floor.

d Ibrahim and Kareem return to the building at two o'clock in the afternoon.

e Kareem goes back inside through the kitchen window.

f Ibrahim phones Omar to get him to come and find the jewellery.

g Omar takes the stolen necklace from under the water around a plant.

h Kareem hears a police radio when he is filming Omar.

WORD WORK

Complete Kareem's diary on page 49 using the words below.

crawled   disaster   drew

knees   footsteps   light bulb

shone   torch   soil

We went to Omar's Internet office building in our cleaners' disguises in the evening. I took the a) .....light bulb..... out of the bathroom to make it dark. I also b) .... a line on the balcony outside Omar's office to help me film him. Then we left. Very early the next morning we came back. My brother Ibrahim helped me to climb up and I went through an open window. I got on my hands and c) .... and d) .... through the building. I hid under a desk in an office. Later I heard e) .... outside the door and the security guard f) .... his g) .... round the room, but he didn't see me. It was nearly a h) .... when Omar went to get the stolen necklace from under the i) .... around one of the plants in the building. I was waiting to film him opening the drawer of his desk.

GUESS WHAT

What happens in the last chapter? Tick four boxes.

a ☐ Kareem's film shows Omar with the jewellery.

b ☐ Kareem takes the film to the police.

c ☐ Kareem takes the film to Sheikh Bin Salem.

d ☐ Kareem takes the film to Samira's father.

e ☐ Omar goes to prison.

f ☐ Omar leaves the country.

g ☐ Kareem and Samira get married.

CHAPTER 8
Fathers

I didn't want to look again. It was too dangerous. If Omar comes out of the bathroom now, he'll see me, I thought. I went on filming. Was Omar still there? I heard a noise. I put my hand in my pocket and pulled out my phone. It was a text message from Ibrahim: 'He's gone.'

Did I want to look at the film? Yes and no. If Omar isn't on the film, I thought, nothing will change. People will say that our father is a thief and that we are the children of a thief. And that will be the end of all our plans. Omar will hide the jewellery in another place or he'll sell it. We'll never find it again.

But now I had no time to look at the film. I had to get out of the building before someone found me. I left the balcony and moved to the stairs. The guard was sitting near the front door. I couldn't leave through the front door or through the bathroom window on the ground floor. But Ibrahim and I had another plan. The night before we decided to leave a bucket and a **rope** in the kitchen. I put the video camera in the bucket and put the rope through the handle. I sent Ibrahim a message on his phone. I wanted him to be near the balcony.

Very slowly and carefully I **lowered** the bucket down from the balcony to Ibrahim. It wasn't easy. But soon the bucket was in his hands. Now for me. I couldn't jump down. The balcony was too high. But there was another window on the stairs. I could jump from there. I went back to the stairs and climbed through the window. It was a small window and difficult to get through, but I did it. Then I jumped and hit the ground. Slowly, I stood up. My knees and hands hurt, but I could walk.

'Did you see the jewellery? Did you film Omar with it?' asked Ibrahim as he helped me to stand.

rope a very thick string

lower to make something go down

I didn't answer him. I just wanted to get away. We ran around the side of the building and towards my car. I felt more comfortable when we were inside it, and driving home again.

'Did he open the drawer? Was the jewellery inside?' my brother asked again.

'It wasn't in the drawer. It was in the soil around one of the plants in another office!' I said to a surprised Ibrahim. 'And I don't know if Omar's on the film.'

'Well there's only one way to find out. Let's look at the film,' he said, as we jumped out of the car and hurried through the **gate** into our house. We watched the film worriedly. There was the jewellery on the desk. But there was nobody in the room. Still nobody. Where are you, Omar? Where are you? I thought. And then we saw him. He walked towards the desk, took the jewellery in his hand and put it in his pocket.

'That's it. We've got him,' I shouted.

There could be no **doubt**. Omar was the thief. We turned the film off. We were so happy. We **hugged** each other.

'But honestly, Ibrahim, I don't know what to do now. We can't just walk into any police station. Omar's from an important family. Perhaps the police won't listen to us. But first, I must ring Samira and tell her the news.'

The phone rang only once before she answered it.

'I'm so happy. I've counted the minutes, waiting for your call. This is wonderful, but I think you're right. You can't just take it to any police station. They won't believe you. Bring it to our house and show it to my father. He'll know what to do. The police will listen to him.'

She was right. He was Minister of Telecommunications – an important man. But I wasn't happy about going to his house.

'He doesn't like me, or my family, any more,' I told Samira.

'He wanted you as a **son-in-law**, but it was difficult for him. I know he'll be pleased now,' she said quietly.

gate a door in a garden

doubt when you are not sure about something

hug to put your arms around someone

son-in-law the man who is married to your daughter

I smiled to myself as we drove to Samira's house. 'I'm going to marry her,' I said to myself. 'Nobody's going to stop us.'

But first the world must know the truth about my father. We arrived at Samira's house. The gates were open and Samira's father was waiting for us at the front door.

'Samira has told me this story. Has Omar Bin Salem stolen from his parents? It's difficult to believe. But I always believed that your father was a good man so I'm going to look at your film. Come with me.'

We followed him into a large room. There was a large, white sofa and some very comfortable, low chairs. In front of us there was a big television screen with a **video player** under it. Samira's father took our film and put it in the video player. He sat back and turned the television on. I didn't watch the film again. I was looking at his face. He moved closer to the

*I was looking
at his face.*

television. Then he stopped the film. He watched it again. He stopped the film again and turned off the television. Then he spoke to us.

'This is terrible and wonderful. It's wonderful for your father, but Ahmed Bin Salem is also a good and honest man. After he sees this film, he'll never be the same. How did you get it?'

I didn't want to tell him. He was Samira's father, but I wasn't ready to tell him everything.

'It's OK, son,' he smiled, 'You don't have to tell me all your secrets. I know I **broke off** your engagement to Samira. I'm sure I'm not your favourite person. But everyone makes mistakes, son. I was wrong.'

I liked that word 'son'.

'I have to show this to Omar's father first,' he went on. 'You don't know how terrible this is. It's going to kill him. But everyone must know the truth. Your father has great sons – and I have a wonderful daughter. Her phone's been very busy this week, more than usual. Now I know why,' he smiled. 'Now go and tell your father the good news.'

⌒〰⌒

This happened four years ago. Samira and I got married a year later. Her father gave us a beautiful, big house as a wedding present. My father is still working for Sheikh Ahmed Bin Salem. After he saw the film, Sheikh Bin Salem put **advertisements** in all the newspapers in the country. The advertisements talked about father's **honesty** and hard work, and Sheikh Bin Salem gave my father an even better job. And Omar? Nobody talks about Omar. He left the country and hasn't come back. His father closed Omar's company and sold everything in the office. Omar's two younger brothers are now working with their father. And the bad times? They weren't all bad. Because of them, I now know that I have the best wife in the world.

break off (*past* **broke**, **broken**) to stop

advertisement you pay to put this information in the newspaper

honesty not stealing

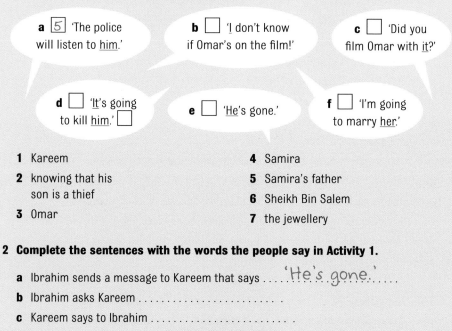

READING CHECK

1 Who or what are the underlined words?

a ⑤ 'The police will listen to <u>him</u>.'

b ☐ 'I don't know if Omar's on the film!'

c ☐ 'Did you film Omar with <u>it</u>?'

d ☐ '<u>It</u>'s going to kill <u>him</u>.' ☐

e ☐ '<u>He</u>'s gone.'

f ☐ 'I'm going to marry <u>her</u>.'

1 Kareem	**4** Samira
2 knowing that his son is a thief	**5** Samira's father
	6 Sheikh Bin Salem
3 Omar	**7** the jewellery

2 Complete the sentences with the words the people say in Activity 1.

a Ibrahim sends a message to Kareem that says .... *'He's gone.'* ....

b Ibrahim asks Kareem ....

c Kareem says to Ibrahim ....

d .... Samira says to Kareem.

e Samira's father says to Kareem ....

f .... says Kareem to himself.

WORD WORK

Complete the sentences on page 55 with the words from the video camera.

advertisements   doubt
breaking off   gates   hugs
honesty   lowers   rope
son-in-law   video player

a There is no .... doubt .... that Omar was the thief.

b After filming Omar, Kareem puts a video camera in the bucket and then he puts a .... through the handle of a bucket.

c After that he .... the video camera down to Ibrahim.

d When they see the film of Omar with the stolen jewellery, Kareem .... Ibrahim.

e The .... of Samira's house are open when Kareem and Ibrahim arrive there.

f They watch the video again on a .... at Samira's house.

g When Samira's father knows that Kareem's father is not a thief, he is happy to have Kareem as his ....

h He says sorry to Kareem for .... his engagement with Samira.

i Sheikh Bin Salem puts .... in all the newspapers to say that Kareem's father was a good man.

j The video of Omar with the stolen necklace proves the .... of Kareem's father.

GUESS WHAT

Imagine that it is five years after the end of the story. Which of these do you think has happened?

a ☐ Kareem and Samira have two children.

b ☐ Omar is making a lot of money on the Internet in America.

c ☐ Ibrahim is a police officer.

d ☐ Kareem's father is working with Samira's father.

Project A *A country in the Middle East*

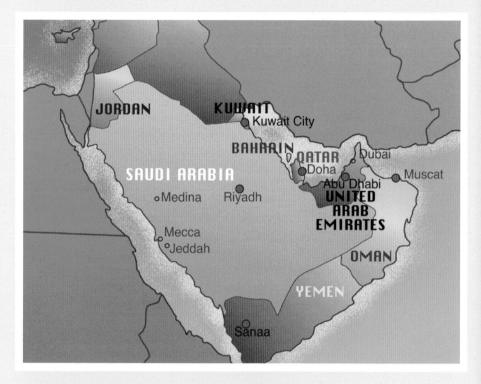

1 Read the text and complete the information table on page 57.

The United Arab Emirates are in the Middle East next to Oman and Saudi Arabia. The capital is Abu Dhabi. The UAE are 82,880 square kilometres in size, and they became independent on 2 December 1971. Arabic is the official language, but people speak Persian, English, Hindi, and Urdu there, too. The UAE export oil, natural gas, dried fish and dates. People from the United Arab Emirates are called Emiratis. The Emirati Internet code is .ae and there were 900,000 Internet users in the UAE in 2002. The population of the UAE was just over three million in 2000, and one million people in the country had mobile phones in 1999.

NAME:	EXPORTS:
CAPITAL:	
AREA: sq km	POPULATION:
LANGUAGES:	INTERNET COUNTRY CODE:
	INTERNET USERS:
INDEPENDENCE:	PEOPLE WITH MOBILE PHONES:
NATIONALITY:	

2 Look at the tables and write about another country. Use the text about the United Arab Emirates to help you.

NAME: Sultanate of Oman	EXPORTS: oil, natural gas, cement, copper
CAPITAL: Muscat	
AREA: 212,460 sq km	POPULATION: 2,533,389 (2000)
LANGUAGES: Arabic, English, Urdu, and Indian languages	INTERNET COUNTRY CODE: .om
	INTERNET USERS: 120,000 (2002)
INDEPENDENCE: 1650	PEOPLE WITH MOBILE PHONES: 52,822 (1997)
NATIONALITY: Omani	

NAME: Jordan	EXPORTS: chemicals, food
CAPITAL: Amman	
AREA: 89,213 sq km	POPULATION: 4,998,564 (2000)
LANGUAGES: Arabic	INTERNET COUNTRY CODE: .jo
	INTERNET USERS: 87,500 (2000)
INDEPENDENCE: 1946	PEOPLE WITH MOBILE PHONES: 75,000 (1999)
NATIONALITY: Jordanian	

Project B *Filming the story*

1 **Write the film words with the correct definitions. Use a dictionary to help you.**

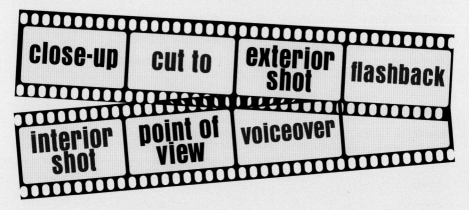

close-up   cut to   exterior shot   flashback

interior shot   point of view   voiceover

a . . . . when we hear someone's voice recorded on top of the sounds of a scene

b . . . . when an outside scene is filmed

c . . . . when an inside scene is filmed

d . . . . when we see a scene that someone remembers from the past

e . . . . when we see something through the eyes of one of the people in a scene

f . . . . when we see something very near, filling the whole cinema screen

g . . . . when we move quickly from one scene to another scene

2 **Use the words in Activity 1 to complete part of a film scene from Chapter 4 of the story.**

(a) . . . . *of the Eastern Trading Company building. Kareem is waiting outside, looking at his watch.*

(b) . . . . *on Kareem's watch. It is ten past twelve.*

From Kareem's **(c)** . . . . *we see Abu Malek walking down the street. We see Abu Malek and Kareem shake hands.*

KAREEM   Can I speak to you about my father?

ABU MALEK   Of course.

(d) . . . . *a café.* **(e)** . . . . *Abu Malek and Kareem are sitting at a table, talking.*

ABU MALEK   I'm angry about what people are saying. I liked your father. People say that he's a thief. They're wrong. Your father's a good man. When my wife was sick, he helped me. He gave me money to buy her what she needed. He's a kind man.

KAREEM   Thank you. My father needs help now. He travelled to Dubai last Friday. I need to know what happened the day before he went. Who went to my father's office? Can you remember?

ABU MALEK   Let me think for a while. Last Thursday . . .

In **(f)** . . . . *we see what Abu Malek remembers and describes. His voice continues in* **(g)** . . . .

ABU MALEK   Yes, now I remember . . . I went into your father's office four or five times to take him a cup of coffee. I do that every day.

3   Look back at pages 23–24 of Chapter 4 and order these parts of the flashback scene. Number them 1–9.

a ☐ Khaled Mansoor comes back to his office at 4 o'clock.

b ☐ Khaled Mansoor goes to Sheikh Bin Salem's office to speak to him.

c ☐ Khaled Mansoor leaves his office for lunch.

d ☐ Mr Moussa goes into Khaled Mansoor's office.

e ☐ Mr Nasser goes into Khaled Mansoor's office.

f ☐ Mr Nasser leaves Khaled Mansoor's office.

g ☐ Omar Bin Salem arrives looking for his father.

h ☐ Sheikh Bin Salem leaves the office.

i ☐ Two visitors from Jordan visit Khaled Mansoor.

4 Write a different film scene from the story. Use one of these pictures to help you.

GRAMMAR CHECK

Reported speech with that clauses

After the verbs *forget, hear, know, remember, think, explain,* and *agree* we can use that + a reported speech clause (subject + verb + the rest of the sentence). The tense in the reported speech clause must agree with the main verb. We must make changes in pronouns and possessive adjectives, too.

'Kareem is one of our best students,' think the teachers.

Kareem's teachers think that he's one of their best students.

'This isn't my parcel,' I explained.

I explained that it wasn't my parcel.

Remember the past tense of the modal verbs *will (would), can (could), must (had to).*

'We'll think about what to do next,' we agreed.

We agreed that we would think about what to do next.

1 Write the sentences again. Use reported speech with *that*.

a 'I want to marry Samira because she is clever and beautiful,' explained Kareem.

Kareem explained that he wanted to marry Samira because she was clever and beautiful.

b 'We were so happy to hear about our father's new job,' Kareem remembered.

....

....

c 'We will meet Samira's family,' Kareem's father agreed.

....

....

d 'There will be an announcement about our engagement on Saturday,' Samira heard.

....

....

e 'I have some important business for the owner,' Kareem's father explained.

....

....

f 'Perhaps there has been a car accident,' Kareem's mother thought.

....

....

GRAMMAR CHECK

Indefinite pronouns

We use indefinite pronouns to refer in general to people, things, or places without giving specific details.

people	things	places	
someone	something	somewhere	There was a phone call from someone who knew Samira's father.
no one	nothing	nowhere	There was no one in the office.
everyone	everything	everywhere	Kareem loves everything about Samira.
anyone	anything	anywhere	They couldn't find the necklace or the earrings anywhere.

2 Complete Kareem's father's story. Use indefinite pronouns.

'About two weeks ago a) ..*someone*.. stole some jewellery from Sheikh Bin Salem's house. I didn't know it, but some of the jewellery was in a parcel. There was a note asking me to take the parcel b) .... in Dubai. When I got there c) .... was waiting to take the parcel.

'Soon after that, the police arrested me. I had to wait at the police station for a long time and d) .... told me e) .... I told the policeman that I didn't know f) .... about the jewellery. The policeman knew g) .... about me – my address, my job, my family. I was worried that h) .... would happen to you all.

'I've worked for Sheikh Bin Salem for a long time. i) .... like this has ever happened before. He asked me to take the parcel because he trusted me more than j) .... else. But now he can't trust me and k) .... will think that I am the thief. Perhaps the police will find l) .... to help them to catch the true thief. Then I can forget all this.'

GRAMMAR CHECK

Past Simple: subject and object questions

When the question word (Who or What) is the object of a Past Simple question, we use the auxiliary verb did + infinitive without *to*.

Who did you see? (*who* is the object; *you* is the subject)

What did he do? (*what* is the object; *he* is the subject)

When the question word is the subject of the question, we do not use *did*.

Who went to my father's office? (*who* is the subject)

What happened after that? (*what* is the subject)

3 **Write questions using the Past Simple form of the verbs in brackets. Then underline the subject of each question.**

a what / Kareem's father / for Abu Malek? (do)

   What did <u>Kareem's father</u> do for Abu Malek?

b who / tea / in the morning? (drink)

   ....

c who / Abu Malek / coffee for? (make)

   ....

d what / at lunchtime? (happen)

   ....

e who / Kareem's father's office / in the afternoon? (visit)

   ....

f what / Kareem's father and Sheikh Bin Salem / about? (laugh)

   ....

g who / the building / first? (leave)

   ....

h who / at the office / at nine o'clock? (arrive)

   ....

i who / Omar / for? (look)

   ....

GRAMMAR CHECK

Present Perfect and Past Simple

We use the Present Perfect to talk about things happening at some time in the past without saying when.

I've been a visitor there many times.

We can also use the Present Perfect + *for/since* to talk about things that began in the past and are continuing now.

Abu Malek has been with the company for a long time. (for + a period of time)

Omar's brothers have worked with their father since that day. (since = from a point in past time to now)

We use the Past Simple to talk about things that happened at a specific time in the past and that are now finished.

Samira rang me at breakfast time.

4 **Complete the sentences. Use the Present Perfect or Past Simple of the verbs in brackets.**

a That evening I Knocked. on the door of my father's office. (knock)

b The cleaners are from Pakistan, but they .... here for three years. (live)

c The maids .... for him since they arrived in the country. (work)

d The police .... through their things earlier but they .... anything. (look, not find)

e Last year we .... a new office in Dubai. It .... an expensive year for the Sheikh. (open, be)

f A year ago Sheikh Bin Salem .... Omar the money that he .... to set up his business. (give, need)

g Perhaps Omar .... the jewellery away, or perhaps he .... it. It could be anywhere now. (throw, sell)

h Samira .... me later that day. (phone)

i The driver .... the cleaners at lunchtime and .... them to work for Samira's sister. (find, ask)

GRAMMAR CHECK

be + adjective + –ing form verb/infinitive with to

We can talk about when someone is in the middle of doing something using the verb be + adjective + –ing form of the verb. In these sentences, the adjective is a result of the activity.

The guard was busy talking to his friend.

Kareem's father was happy working for Sheikh Ahmed Bin Salem.

We can describe people's feelings about an action using the verb be + adjective + infinitive with *to*.

They were lucky to have help.   *It's wrong to steal.*

5 Complete the sentences. Use the correct form of the verbs in the box.

be	do	get into	go	put	see	sleep
start	suspect	take	watch	wait	work	

a We must be careful ..to put.. things back in the same place.

b The man was alone .... late at the office.

c It will be difficult .... a photo of Omar's desk because he'll see the flash from the camera.

d Kareem was happy .... his car and go home.

e Kareem and Ibrahim were bored .... the cleaning for two nights.

f If someone is working late, it will be hard .... up to the first floor.

g Kareem wasn't comfortable .... under the desk.

h It won't be easy .... the open window if the bathroom is dark.

i Kareem was cold .... on the balcony.

j Kareem was busy .... Omar and he forgot to film him.

k It was stupid .... afraid, but Kareem thought that the police car was coming for him.

l They were right .... Omar. He was the thief!

GRAMMAR CHECK

Modal auxiliary verbs: must and need to

We use must + infinitive without *to* when it is an obligation to do something.

We must find a way to help our father.

We use must not (mustn't) + infinitive without *to* when it is an obligation not to do something.

We mustn't talk to the security guard.

We use need + to + infinitive to say that an action is necessary.

We need to photograph him holding the jewellery.

We use don't need + to + infinitive or needn't + infinitive without *to* to say that an action is not necessary.

We don't need to look in all the cupboards.

We needn't look in all the cupboards.

Note that *must* has no future form. The future form of *need to* is *will need to.*

6 Choose the correct verbs to complete the sentences.

a Samira and Ibrahim have done their jobs very well. Now Kareem **must**/needn't do the same.

b You **don't need/needn't** to visit the office during the day. You can climb into the building late at night.

c If something goes wrong tonight, we'll **need to/must** come back.

d We haven't got much time. We **must/needn't** work quickly.

e I don't want trouble for my parents. The security guard **mustn't/needn't** see me.

f Samira **needs/must** to phone Omar and tell him that she knows that he's got the jewellery.

g Kareem **doesn't need/mustn't** wait for Omar in his office. He **needs/must** hide on the balcony.

h Kareem **needn't/mustn't** watch out for Omar's car because that's Ibrahim's job.

i When Kareem was filming he was thinking, 'Omar **mustn't/needs to** see me!'

GRAMMAR CHECK

First conditional

We use the first conditional to talk about something that will happen in the future as a result of an action or condition in the present or in the future. We can put the *if* clause at the beginning of the sentence: If + Present Simple, + will/won't + infinitive without *to*. In this case, we use a comma after the *if* clause.

If the security guard finds me, I'll be in a lot of trouble.

We can also put the *if* clause at the end of the sentence. In this case, we do not use a comma.

I'll be in a lot of trouble if the security guard finds me.

7 Complete the sentences. Use the correct form of the verbs in brackets.

a If Kareem ..*films*.. Omar with the jewellery, it ..*will prove*.. that he's the thief. (film, prove)

b If Kareem .... Omar with the jewellery, Omar .... that Kareem put it in his office. (not film, say)

c Everyone .... that Kareem is a thief like his father if the guards .... him in the office. (say, find)

d If Kareem .... in the building, someone .... him. (stay, find)

e Omar .... Kareem if he .... out of the bathroom now. (see, come)

f Nothing .... if Omar and the jewellery .... on the film. (change, not be)

g If Kareem and Ibrahim .... to the police, they .... them. (go, not believe)

h If they .... Samira's father, he .... what to do. (tell, know)

i If Sheikh Bin Salem .... this film, he .... very angry with Omar. (see, be)

DOMINOES Your Choice

Read *Dominoes* for pleasure, or to develop language skills. It's your choice.

Each *Domino* reader includes:
- a good story to enjoy
- integrated activities to develop reading skills and increase vocabulary
- task-based projects – perfect for CEFR portfolios
- contextualized grammar activities

Each *Domino* pack contains a reader, and an excitingly dramatized audio recording of the story

If you liked this *Domino*, read these:

Saladin
Nina Prentice

'Well, Yusuf, are you sure that you want to be a soldier?'
'I'll do my best, Uncle.'
When Yusuf went to Aleppo to learn to fight under General Shirkuh, no one knew what this young man would do with his life.
But years later, Yusuf became the great and chivalrous general, Saladin – the man who helped to bring Muslims together to win back the holy city of Jerusalem from the Franks. This is his story . . .

Green Planet
Christine Lindop

Once 'green' was just a colour. Now we use it to talk about a way of looking at our world and thinking about the environment. But how green is our planet today?
From nuclear power plants to Nemo the clownfish, from polar bears to pesticides, from Greenpeace to global warming, this book brings together many different stories that have made environmental history.
Read it, and perhaps you too can help to make our planet greener!

	CEFR	Cambridge Exams	IELTS	TOEFL iBT	TOEIC
Level 3	B1	PET	4.0	57-86	550
Level 2	A2–B1	KET-PET	3.0-4.0	–	390
Level 1	A1–A2	YLE Flyers/KET	3.0	–	225
Starter & Quick Starter	A1	YLE Movers	1.0–2.0	–	–

You can find details and a full list of books and teachers' resources on our website:
www.oup.com/elt/gradedreaders